WINDOW
ON THE
GREAT WESTERN

An Album of Everyday Scenes from the 1930s & 40s

M. F. YARWOOD

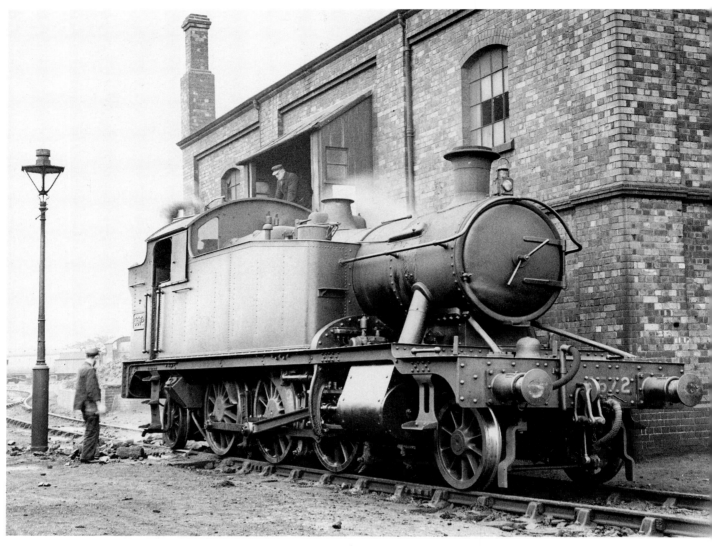

Now preserved at Didcot Railway Centre, 2–6–2 Tank No. 5572 stands beside the coaling stage at Stafford Road Depot, Wolverhampton. Amongst its duties at Kidderminster would have been local passenger trips on the Worcester, Wolverhampton and Severn Valley lines. (11th September 1934)

Previous page: No. 5029 *Nunney Castle* coasting out of Sonning Cutting towards its Reading stop with the 2.15 p.m. Paddington to Cheltenham Express. Shedded throughout its Great Western career at Old Oak Common, the engine took this train as far as Gloucester. The train itself was fairly light, with just six coaches for Cheltenham, and a further two at the rear for Swindon; hardly a taxing load for a 'Castle'. Built in 1934, *Nunney Castle* was withdrawn from service in December 1963 and sold to Woodhams, Barry Docks, from where it was rescued in 1976 for restoration by the Great Western Society at Didcot. (19th August 1948)

Designed by Paul Karau
Typeset by Berkshire Publishing Services
Printed by Amadeus Press Ltd., Huddersfield

Published by
WILD SWAN PUBLICATIONS LTD.
1-3 Hagbourne Road, Didcot, Oxon OX11 8DP

INTRODUCTION

THERE is no doubt that old photographs, whatever the subject, have a peculiar fascination. Interest in them has grown enormously in recent years and in no case more than that of railway subjects. In the last thirty years or so the railways of Britain have undergone vast changes, one result of which has been the development of a widespread nostalgia for the now bygone era of steam, semaphore signals, and wayside stations. Nowadays old railway photographs are scrutinised, not only for the main subject but for the background detail in an effort to recapture the ambience of the period. It is with this in mind that I hope that this selection of photographs will refresh the memories of older readers and stimulate the interest of those who have grown up since the Age of Steam.

The photographs are arranged in chronological order (with just a few exceptions), the first taken in 1932 and the last ones in 1949, by which time the Great Western Railway Company had become part of the nationalised British Railways although there was, as yet, little evidence of change. There are none for the war period 1940-45 when there was a ban on railway photography and my interests had perforce to lie in other directions. On the subject of dates, I have always made a point of recording the location and date of my photos, adding the time of day when it seemed relevant. This has been of great value in the interpretation of the pictures and I strongly recommend it as good practice — it is surprising how little one remembers of the circumstances after ten years, let alone fifty!

Although this is a collection of Great Western pictures, I am aware that large areas of that great railway are not covered. I can only plead that the limitations of just two weeks holiday a year and a limited amount of pocket money in those days meant that one had to be very selective and, of course, there were other railways to be visited. However, I feel that a good part of the special character of the Great Western Railway is conveyed by the pictures.

This book is, in a way, a commemoration of sixty years of railway photography. I took my first pictures in 1929 — not on the GWR — and, yes, the camera was a Box Brownie. After a brief spell with a very basic 116 Ensign folding camera, in 1932 I acquired a 120-size Ensign Carbine with an f4.5 Aldis lens and a Compur shutter with a top speed of 1/250th second. This was replaced in 1937 by a Rolleiflex, while by 1939 I had succumbed to the attractions of 35mm photography in the shape of a Leica camera, various models of which I have continued to use ever since. I still enjoy in a modest way photographing railway subjects, for there is always something of interest to record, whether it is a new development or the vanishing vestiges of abandoned lines, obsolescent stock and the like. One must always remember that the commonplace scenes of today may become rarities all too soon.

M. F. YARWOOD
1989

A classic study of 'Bulldog' No. 3358 *Tremayne* standing at the entrance to the old workshops at Stafford Road, Wolverhampton. This engine was one of the early group of 'Bulldogs' with combined name and numberplates on the cabsides (41 in all), the first twenty-one having curved frames, and the remainder straight. Like many of her class, she was moved around a great deal, being at Chippenham and Weymouth in 1902, Newton Abbot and Plymouth in 1914, followed by a decade in the Worcester and Gloucester Districts during the 'twenties. During the latter part of her career, she saw service mostly on the Crewe line from Wellington, though with periods at Chester and Banbury in between. She was withdrawn from service in late 1945. (14th August 1933)

'655' Class 0—6—0PT No. 1741 by the coaling stage at Stafford Road shed. Built in 1892, she was withdrawn in 1938 and sold to the Amalgamated Anthracite Collieries in South Wales. She spent nearly the whole of her working life within the northern area, a significant portion of which involved working on the Crewe line. Her last few years were spent in the Worcester District. (14th August 1933)

'2021' Class 0—6—0PT No. 2032, fresh from overhaul at Stafford Road. Originally a saddle tank, No. 2032 received her panniers in 1922. Having spent nearly all of her first quarter-century of service at Lydney, she was moved to the Central Wales Division in 1924 where she remained until her demise in 1951. No. 2032 was one of a number of the class fitted with an enclosed cab. (14th August 1933)

Crane loco No. 17 *Cyclops* at Stafford Road Depot on 14th August 1933. No. 17 had been employed at Stafford Road Works for many years, but not long after this photograph was taken, it was transferred to Swindon where it was withdrawn from service in the autumn of 1936.

'517' Class 0—4—2T No. 1442 at Stafford Road on 14th August 1933. Still fitted with a round-topped firebox, she was awaiting overhaul, and would return to service with a Belpaire-type boiler a few months later. Built in January 1878, she survived until 1945, having covered most of the Great Western system in her time. She was at Wells at the turn of the century, Worcester, Stratford and Kidderminster in 1914, before moving across to Tyseley and Stourbridge. As an auto-fitted engine, she spent the years 1927 to 1932 stationed at Banbury and Aylesbury, working on the Bicester and Kingham lines. Her auto gear was removed in 1932 as she was moved to Stafford Road shed, moving on to Ludlow and Shrewsbury thereafter. Her last ten years of service were spent at Swindon, being withdrawn in 1945.

Outside Oxley Depot, Wolverhampton, 'Castle' Class No. 4000 *North Star*, ready for the road, is seen in the company of a line of locomotives, headed by Collett 0—6—0 No. 2256, awaiting repairs at Stafford Road Works. *North Star* was rebuilt as a 'Castle' in 1929, being an Old Oak engine by the time of this photograph. She moved to Shrewsbury in 1934 and to Stafford Road in 1939, where she remained until Nationalisation. The Collett Goods was from the neighbouring Stafford Road shed. (14th August 1933)

Whilst a few of the Wolverhampton-built '850' Class engines retained their saddle tanks throughout their lives, No. 2004 did not. She was, however, the last but one to receive panniers, in 1935. Built in 1892, she survived for sixty years, spending her life almost entirely at sheds between the Birmingham area and Birkenhead. This photograph shows her inside the round-house shed at Shrewsbury on 20th August 1933.

Collett designed his '58XX' Class 0—4—2 Tanks for branch and shunting duties, but, unlike their more numerous '48XX' Class brethren, they were not fitted for auto-train working. No. 5811, a Wellington-based engine, is seen here at Stafford Road on 14th August 1933, when new. She, and her sister engine No. 5810, worked on the Craven Arms branch for a short spell at this period. No. 5811 was moved to Bala in 1934, being followed by the other engine the following year. Their duties were taken over by 44XX class locomotives.

'Metro' tank No. 3569 in its final form with large water tanks, an enlarged coal bunker (still retaining the so-called Wolverhampton backplate), and an ATC trip valve for working over electrified lines in the London Area. She spent very many years at Slough, and latterly at Southall whose shed code she still carries (SHL), stencilled on the bunker front plate. Having moved to Shrewsbury during 1932, she was photographed at that shed on 20th August 1933. Her last two years of service were spent at Birkenhead, being withdrawn in March 1936.

'Mogul' No. 4387 from St. Philip's Marsh shed, Bristol, approaching Birmingham Snow Hill with a train of local stock on Saturday, 26th August 1933. The leading four coaches form a Birmingham Division Standard 'B' Set, forty-eight of which operated the bulk of the Birmingham area's suburban services. Two extra Thirds bring up the rear on what might be the 1.10 p.m. (Saturdays only) train to Leamington Spa. The single lamp on the centre of the engine's bufferbeam would normally signify a light engine, or engine and brake van, but a certain number of local trains running on the main line between Wolverhampton, Birmingham and Leamington Spa were noted thus.

Shrewsbury 'Star' No. 4058 *Princess Augusta* entering Snow Hill station with the 11.00 a.m. Shrewsbury to Paddington parcels train. The first eight vehicles are empty stock, and include a Royal Mail van, all possibly destined for Swindon? The rear half of the train is the 'Parcels' proper, and consists of brake vans and Siphon G's destined for Paddington, Plymouth, Weymouth and Neyland in addition to one for Birmingham itself. More vehicles would be added to the train during its twenty-minute stop at Snow Hill. (4th September 1934)

A 'Dudley Moke' awaiting departure time at Snow Hill's platform 4. The locomotive is '517' Class 0–4–2T No. 1466, built at Wolverhampton in 1883, and the Auto trailer, the 76-seater No. 70. The much-travelled locomotive is nearing the end of its days. Amongst its duties during its long life were the Helston, Brixham, Teign Valley, Marlborough, and Abingdon branches, and in 1933/4, the Banbury and Kingham service. After a short stay at Stafford Road (during which time it operated the Dudley service), No. 1466 moved to Weymouth, from whence it was withdrawn from service, in July 1935. (4th September 1934)

At the north end of Snow Hill station, Prairie tank No. 5167 brings empty stock towards Platform 11 to form the 12.47 p.m. stopping train to Leamington Spa. The stock is one of the Divisional 'A' sets comprising four 63ft vehicles, and seating 360 passengers. No. 5167 is one of Leamington's stud of seven 51XX tanks. On the Up Through line is 45XX tank No. 4579, pulling hard up the gradient of 1 in 50 with a transfer freight to Bordesley Junction. This engine had been stationed at Tyseley since new in March 1927, but would be 'transferred' within a month or two to Pembroke Dock. (7th September 1934)

'Bulldog' 4—4—0 No. 3380 *River Yealm* passing through Birmingham Snow Hill on the down middle road on Friday, 7th September 1934, with a horse-box special. As the engine is from Didcot shed, there is a very strong probability that the 'boxes originated from Lambourn, and that they are heading for the Manchester Race Meeting. Manchester traditionally held a Flat Meeting in early September, and specials were scheduled on the days before race days; thus, the horses being conveyed would run on the Saturday. The specials were routed via Wellington and Crewe, traditionally leaving Lambourn at around 8.00 a.m. and arriving at Brindle Heath about 3.15 p.m. It was customary to provide a Brake Compo for the stable staff travelling with the horses, and we see a coach marshalled toward the rear of the train. 'A' headlamps were mandatory for such trains.

Built at Wolverhampton in 1899, '2021' Class 0–6–0PT No. 2061 is seen here at Stafford Road. Having spent long spells at Chester and Stourbridge Junction sheds, the engine was allocated to Birkenhead during 1932/3. It was at the latter location that the necessity for the warning bell arose, as the locomotive would certainly have found employment within the Dock area. Some twelve months after leaving Birkenhead, she still retains the bell. No. 2061 was to spend the lion's share of her remaining twenty years' service at Wolverhampton. (11th September 1934)

Shortly before withdrawal, Armstrong 'Standard Goods' No. 1195 stands at her home shed, Oxley. Built at Swindon in April 1876, the engine was given a Belpaire firebox in 1901. By 1934, only two of the class remained, No. 1094 at Stourbridge Junction, and 1195. No. 1094 went in March of that year, whilst 1195 remained in service until October, the last of her class of 310 engines. (11th September 1934)

Now preserved at Didcot Railway Centre, 56XX 0–6–2 Tank No. 6697 stands forlorn at Oxley shed. Whilst the vast majority of the 200 locomotives of this class were stationed in South Wales, a small number (eleven in 1934) were always associated with sheds in the Wolverhampton Division. Leamington shed had a trio for many years (used frequently on the Honeybourne goods trips) and 6697 was one of them. She arrived at Leamington in 1930, and was still there in the early 'fifties. (11th September 1934)

'Duke' Class 4—4—0 No. 3264 *Trevithick* being prepared for the road at Tyseley Depot. Driver C. Malpass is doing the final round with his oilcan before setting off, probably to take the 1.15 p.m. stopping train from Snow Hill to Wellington. *Trevithick* was a Cambrian section engine at this time, being shedded at Aberystwyth. In 1938 she moved to Gloucester, ending her working life in that area in 1949. (14th September 1934)

Awaiting attention outside the repair shop at Tyseley, 'Bulldog' Class No. 3450 *Peacock* stands minus her coupling rod. The absence of the rod shows up the deep frame, which was a feature of the last batch of 15 'Bulldogs' built in 1909/10. A resident of Tyseley shed, her duties would have been mainly on the local passenger services on the Stratford, Leamington and Wolverhampton lines. A rather 'footloose' locomotive, she was allocated to at least ten different sheds during the Grouping period, within an area bounded by Reading, Weston-Super-Mare, Hereford and Chester. This was, however, by no means uncommon for the 'Bulldogs'. (14th September 1934)

Visiting Oxley shed on 11th September 1934 is a Wrexham (Croes Newydd) 'Aberdare', No. 2679. Completed in December 1902, she was the penultimate engine of her class, and survived until early 1946 at Worcester. When new, the class were shared mainly between Aberdare and Swindon sheds, but worked coal trains from such points as Llantrisant and Rogerstone, too. They were gradually superseded on the heavier coal trains by 28XX locomotives, and as a result were distributed over a wider area. Even so, they continued to be associated with mineral traffic.

One of the 'Night Owls'! Old Oak Common 47XX Class 2–8–0 No. 4705 stands at Tyseley shed awaiting her next turn of duty, an overnight fast vacuum freight to London. Tyseley itself had a pair of these engines to cover the balancing workings, and Old Oak locomotives. Their loads normally consisted of 60-70 vehicles running under 'C' class lamps, with not less than a third of the train consisting of vacuum wagons with their pipes connected to the engine. (14th September 1934)

Driver C. Thomas poses beside his charge, Churchward 28XX 2—8—0 No. 2874, at Tyseley on 14th September 1934. This engine was shedded at Tyseley at this time, and is probably being prepared for one of the London freights from the neighbouring Bordesley Junction yard. Some of these were Southall-bound, conveying 60 wagons as far as Banbury, and 100 beyond. No. 2874 was built in 1918, spending its early years at various London Division sheds. It arrived at Tyseley from Leamington shed in 1930, moving on to Neath in 1936.

ROD Class 2—8—0 No. 3033 taking water at Oxley. Built by the North British Loco Company (to a design of the Great Central Railway) for the Railway Operating Division of the War Department in 1918, it was purchased by the GWR in 1925 and allotted the number 3057. After temporary withdrawal and subsequent overhaul at Swindon, it was returned to service in late 1926 as No. 3033. Allocated initially to Exeter, the engine moved north in 1931, spending about four years at Oxley before being re-allocated to Severn Tunnel Junction in 1936. Although to some extent 'Great Westernised', it was still carrying a GC type chimney when recorded on 11th September 1934.

Another ROD 2—8—0, this one No. 3024, which could well be called 'Oxley's Own'. She was purchased in 1925 and sent to Oxley, and after over-haul returned there in July 1926 for a continuous allocation which lasted beyond Great Western days. 3024 is seen here at her home shed sporting a Taff Vale chimney, as fitted to the Class 'A' 0—6—2T locos. It has also retained the mounting brackets on its smokebox for the Westinghouse brake pump, originally fitted to all the ROD locomotives. She survived until 1958. (13th June 1935)

A further example of William Dean's final freight locomotive design, the 'Aberdare'. With its double frames, small wheels and a pony truck with inside bearings, the engine presented a rather odd appearance. No. 2650 is fitted with a standard Dean 3,000-gallon tender, and was photographed at Oxley on 13th June 1935, just a year before her withdrawal. Her last years were spent at Stourbridge Junction shed.

No. 2674 was allocated to Reading when new, in November 1902. Her first duties, the Reading and Rogerstone coal trains, had been the subject of some heated exchanges between the London Division Traffic Department, and Swindon. When the train exceeded 45 wagons (as it frequently did), it was not possible to place it in a refuge siding, and as a consequence, delays were caused within the Division when an 'Aberdare' and its long train were present. London concluded: 'There is no necessity for the Big Engines to work this side of Swindon'! No. 2674, however, survived the controversy and is recorded here at Oxley shortly before her withdrawal. The 4,000-gallon tender has been transferred from a scrapped ROD, replacing the standard 3,000-gallon type originally fitted. Her last three years were spent at Chester, ending in September 1935. (13th June 1935)

'Star' Class 4—6—0 No. 4025 *Italian Monarch* on the turntable at Stafford Road. Built at Swindon in 1909, she originally carried the name *King Charles*. She was renamed in 1927, along with the rest of the 4021-4030 batch, to clear the series for use on the new 'King' Class engines. At the outbreak of the Second World War, this second name was removed for obvious reasons, and 4025 thereafter ran nameless. In her heyday, she was allocated to Old Oak, then Laira, moving on to such sheds as Newton Abbot, Bath Road, and Exeter in the latter half of the 'twenties as the 'Castle' class increased in numbers. From 1931 onwards, she was allocated variously to Stafford Road, Shrewsbury and Chester. When recorded at Stafford Road, she was a Salop engine, and had worked in on a local passenger from the north, with 'B' headlamps still *in situ*. No. 4025 never received outside steampipes. (13th June 1935)

Taking water at her home shed of Stafford Road, 'Saint' Class 4—6—0 No. 2926 *Saint Nicholas* is being prepared for the next duty, probably a passenger train in the Shrewsbury direction. She had been fitted with a new front end and outside steampipes in 1934. In the early 'twenties, she was still working Welsh expresses between Cardiff and London, and South Wales portions of the 'North and West' trains. A subsequent move to Shrewsbury continued the association with the 'North and West' services, whilst in 1931 she moved to Stafford Road for a prolonged stay. (13th June 1935)

Another thirsty engine is 57XX Class 0—6—0PT No. 5701, seen here taking water at Tyseley on 17th June 1935. The need for light freight and shunting tanks had been satisfied by 1905, and it was not until the late 'twenties that the question of replacing some of the more elderly classes arose. The result was the 57XX class, of which No. 5701 was one of the first 'on duty', being delivered to Tyseley in January 1929. After short allocations to Banbury and Wolverhampton, she returned to Tyseley during 1934 where she stayed for the remainder of her Great Western career, apart from short loans to other divisional sheds. She sports the recently introduced 'shirtbutton' logo.

'Hall' Class 4–6–0 No. 4984 *Albrighton Hall* passing through Bournemouth Central with a Sunday excursion on 1st September 1935, probably from the Midlands, en route to Bournemouth West station. Through working of GWR engines onto the Southern Railway via Basingstoke was very common, and peak traffic periods (such as Bank Holidays) would bring several onto the system. Possibly the Southern, under pressure itself at such times, was unable to provide motive power from Basingstoke for all the excursions, and so some GW locomotives stayed with their trains. The through running was normally to Eastleigh (for Portsmouth-bound trains) or to Bournemouth. No. 4984 is an Old Oak engine, and has probably been 'borrowed' by the shed she was visiting to run the day's return trip.

An August Bank Holiday Saturday excursion near Hinton Admiral (Southern Railway), with Tyseley 'Hall' 4–6–0 No. 4993 *Dalton Hall* in charge. The train is an excursion (hence the number, 079) rather than a strengthening portion of a regular train (number 7XX), and was one of three on that day from the Wolverhampton/Birmingham District to Bournemouth, each hauled by 'Halls'. Note the use of three Birmingham Division suburban sets to form the train, giving seating for over 850 passengers, though unfortunately no lavatory facilities! (31st July 1937)

Another 'Hall', No. 5904 *Kelham Hall* standing outside Bournemouth Central shed, having brought in a 'Newcastle Chronicle' excursion on Whit-Monday, 5th June 1933. Such excursions from the LNE system would normally arrive at Banbury in the early hours of the morning, where the train would be handed over to the GWR for a breakfast-time arrival on the South Coast. No. 5904, stationed at Banbury for about a year in 1933/4, would probably leave later that night with the return trip.

Returning to the Birmingham area with empty stock is another Tyseley 'Hall', No. 4979 *Wootton Hall*, on August Bank Holiday Saturday, 1937. The engine had earlier worked down with an excursion, the identification number for which may be seen under the 'Empty Stock' headboard. The train is seen passing Hinton Admiral (about eight miles east of Bournemouth) with a four-coach divisional set leading a number of clerestory coaches.

'Duke' Class 4–4–0 No. 3285 *Katerfelto* waits at Southampton Terminus station to take out the 4.30 p.m. train to Cheltenham via Andover and the MSWJ line. A basic formation of three coaches on each of the through trains on this line sufficed, although an extra coach was added to some. In addition, the daily through coaches between Southampton and Liverpool were conveyed. No. 3285 was allocated to Cheltenham in 1930, remaining in the area until withdrawal in 1937; she was a familiar sight on the MSWJ during that period, being a Gloucester engine at the time of the photograph.

A period line-up in front of the coaling stage at Exeter shed, the photograph being taken from the Up Relief Platform. On the left is one of the 83XX Class Moguls, No. 8384. These engines were mostly modified 53XX series, with an extended and weighted front buffer-beam area to place extra load onto the pony truck. This would accordingly turn the main frames more on sharp curves, and lessen the serious flange wear being experienced on the front driving wheels. Many were shedded in the West Country, and nearly all were converted back to standard 53XX Class in 1944, No. 8384 becoming her former self, 5384. Collett 48XX Class 0—4—2T No. 4819 was delivered when new to Exeter in April 1933, finding employment mainly on the Teign Valley and Tiverton lines. To her right is '850' Class 0—6—0PT No. 1930, a long-lived engine built in May 1884, which survived until the summer of 1949. On the right of the picture is un-named 'Bulldog' 4—4—0 No. 3361, originally Edward VII (the name being removed in 1927 to avoid duplicaton with the new 'King' Class engine, 6001). All four of these locomotives were allocated to Exeter shed at this time. (4th May 1936)

Newton Abbot shed on 5th May 1936. From left to right are '655' Class 0–6–0PT No. 2709; 'Castle' Class 4–6–0 No. 5026 *Criccieth Castle*; '3150' Class 2–6–2T No. 3161; 'Hall' Class 4–6–0 No. 5913 *Rushton Hall*; '28XX' 2–8–0 No. 2827, and at the extreme right, 0–6–0ST No. 1364. Just in view behind the tender of the 'Castle' may be seen the bunker of '72XX' Class 2–8–2T No. 7202, currently undergoing restoration at the Didcot Railway Centre. Of these engines, the '655', 'Castle' and '1361' were Newton engines, the remainder being visitors. The 'Hall' is a Westbury engine, whilst the '28' was allocated to Severn Tunnel Junction, and had possibly worked down on the 5.15 p.m. Severn Tunnel Junction coal and freight for Newton. Both 3161 and 7202 were from Newport, and had probably worked in on coal trains.

Churchward-Holcroft '1361' Class 0–6–0ST No. 1364 standing on the coal stack siding at Newton Abbot shed. Built at Swindon in 1910 to replace the ageing Cornwall Mineral Railway's design, the class of five engines were permanent residents of the West Country. There were two at Plymouth (Millbay, later Docks), two at Laira, the fifth being at Newton. St. Blazey had an allocation, too, in the early 'twenties. They were constructed primarily for Dock working, but the sharp curvatures found at Newton Abbot required their employment. Sister engine No. 1363 has been preserved by the Great Western Society and is now at Didcot Railway Centre. (5th May 1936)

Another locomotive in which Holcroft had a prominent part in the design was the '43XX' Class. Here, No. 8376, one of the modified locomotives (ex 5376) with a heavy front end accelerates out of Teignmouth station with the 9.28 a.m. Plymouth Millbay to Exeter local. The coach formation is an 'E set', consisting of a van third, lavatory third, and a brake compo, though hardly of matching stock! Its day started with an early return trip from Plymouth to Liskeard, then the 9.28 a.m., after which it returned from Exeter to Kingswear, ending the day at Moretonhampstead. The engine is from Laira shed. (5th May 1936)

Oblivious to the passage of the light engines, two ladies enjoy a constitutional along the sea wall at Teignmouth. 'Hall' 4–6–0 No. 5902 *Howick Hall* from Laira shed, and '43XX' 2–6–0 No. 4379 of St. Philip's Marsh, Bristol, enjoy a constitutional of their own, probably as far as Newton Abbot to pick up their next workings. The '43XX' had only another eighteen months' work ahead of her, before ending up in the Factory 'Pool' at Swindon, from which she was withdrawn early in 1938. (5th May 1936)

An evocative rural GWR scene on the Launceston branch. '2021' Class 0—6—0PT No. 2116 eases into the goods loop at Marsh Mills just after midday with an Up local freight, the 11.30 a.m. from Horrabridge to Laira Junction. No. 2116, a Laira engine, was unusual amongst its class in having a backplate mounted on the rear edge of the bunker, with spectacle glasses, yet retaining its open cab. Note the make-up of the train, with opens in the majority. (7th May 1936)

With No. 2116 safely in the goods yard, a '45XX' Class 2—6—2T arrives at Marsh Mills from the Plymouth direction with the 12.10 p.m. Millbay to Launceston passenger train, consisting of three coaches, and a van attached to the rear. The track to the south of Marsh Mills was double for the short distance to the main line at Tavistock Junction, whose marshalling yard can be seen through the arches of the bridge carrying the A38 trunk road. (7th May 1936)

'28XX' Class 2—8—0 No. 2832 pauses at the stop board at the top of Hemerdon Bank, some six miles to the east of Plymouth, with what is almost certainly the 2.25 a.m. Bristol West Depot to Laira Junction goods, 'J' Class. Just four minutes were allowed at this stop to pin down wagon brakes. The first five vehicles are 'Bloaters', followed by a mixed bag of wagons which may have originated from South Wales, the locomotive being Aberdare-based. (7th May 1936)

By 1936, it was slightly unusual to see a daily Paddington train in this area without at least a 'Castle' 4–6–0 at its head, but, on this occasion, Laira shed has turned out a pair of its lesser mortals to haul the 9.00 a.m. ex-Penzance train, seen here topping Hemerdon Bank. It is probable that both would come off at Newton Abbot to be replaced by a 'King' or 'Castle' for the run to Paddington. There would appear to be some of the recently introduced 'Centenary' stock marshalled about halfway down the train, which is being hauled by 'Hall' 4–6–0 No. 4947 *Nanhoran Hall* and 'Bulldog' 4–4–0 No. 3342 *Bonaventura*. (7th May 1936)

A view of the Royal Albert Bridge, Saltash, which it is no longer possible to take due to the presence of the nearby road bridge. 'Hall' Class 4–6–0 No. 4991 *Cobham Hall* of Truro shed is approaching the eastern portal with a down goods. The line curves through ninety degrees on the Cornwall side, passing through Saltash station, then continues over the Coombe-by-Saltash viaduct which may be seen below the goods train. (8th May 1936)

A lunchtime departure from Plymouth. '49XX' 4—6—0 No. 4957 *Postlip Hall* pulling away from North Road station with the 12.30 p.m. Plymouth Millbay to Newton Abbot local. The 'Hall' is a Truro engine, working through as far as Newton Abbot before returning later with another local to Plymouth. The clerestory composite coach has three third class compartments (leading), and four first class nearest the camera. The antimacassars on the headrests of the first class compartments can be seen, as can the window labels indicating smoking (white rectangle) and non-smoking (red triangle). The proportion between the two is a reversal of modern day trends! (8th May 1936)

'Bulldog' 4—4—0 No. 3393 *Australia* on station pilot duties, at the head of one of the 'B' sets allocated to the Looe branch. Perhaps the set has been brought to Plymouth for attention. No. 3393 herself had arrived at Laira from Cardiff (Canton) shed in 1932, remaining there until 1943 when she was transferred to Worcester. (8th May 1936)

Standing at Liskeard with the 4.00 p.m. from Looe is '45XX' Prairie No. 4543. Unusually, the branch platform was set at right-angles to and remote from the main line station, having its own branch signal box at the northern end of that platform. The signalman/porter may be seen making his way back to the box with the token. Two 'B' sets were allocated to the branch to work the normal services, with two or three additional coaches kept at Liskeard for spares, one of which may be seen on the extreme right-hand edge of the picture. (8th May 1936)

'Bulldog' 4–4–0 No. 3441 *Blackbird* bringing the 4.30 p.m. Taunton to Barnstaple Junction train into South Molton station on Tuesday, 12th May 1936. *Blackbird* spent about a year working on the branch alongside three or four other 'Bulldogs', before returning to Laira. The 'core' of the train is the 'B' set in the centre of the formation, which, during the course of the day, had also worked on the Yeovil and Minehead branches. The leading corridor composite stayed with the 'B' set overnight, working on to Ilfracombe then back to Taunton the following afternoon. The last vehicle is a corridor brake compo, a through coach from London conveyed by the 1.30 p.m. Paddington to Penzance train, detached at Taunton. This coach was worked onwards from Barnstaple Junction to Ilfracombe that evening by the Southern Railway.

Passing Highbridge at speed is 'Castle' 4—6—0 No. 4087 *Cardigan Castle* at the head of the 1.10 p.m. Crewe to Plymouth train. The engine had only recently been returned to the West Country after a spell at Cardiff and Old Oak sheds, and is working through to Newton Abbot with this service. A pair of brake composites head the train, the first working from Liverpool to Kingswear (detached at Newton with the engine), the second from Birkenhead to Plymouth. Then follows a four-coach formation, including dining car, forming the main portion of the train, 12.00 noon from Liverpool (Lime St.) to Plymouth. The penultimate vehicle is another brake compo, this one working from Manchester to Plymouth. Curiously, all of these through vehicles had left their origins within five minutes of each other; Birkenhead at 11.55 a.m., and both Liverpool and Manchester (London Road) at midday. The last coach is a strengthening vehicle. An LMS '3F' 0—6—0 with a milk tank can be seen on the Up main. (14th May 1936)

The LMS '3F' No. 3218 has moved over to the Down Main to allow the passage of an Up freight behind '43XX' 2–6–0 No. 6319. The Mogul is a long way from home, being allocated to Neyland, and is working the 12.42 p.m. Hackney (Newton Abbot) to Avonmouth goods. This engine, like many of her class, had been at sheds all over the system, underlining their general usefulness and versatility. During the Grouping period, 6319 was allocated to sheds as far apart as Wolverhampton, Neyland and Laira. The '3F', carrying a 22E (Highbridge) shed plate, is fitted with Whittaker tablet exchanging apparatus on her tender. (14th May 1936)

One of the later series of '45XX' tanks, No. 5571, bringing the 2.15 p.m. Yeovil (Pen Mill) into Taunton. The 'B' set forming the train was one of about a dozen to be found at Taunton, and which were used on all of the branches radiating from the town. This particular set spent the day working through between Yeovil and Minehead. After spending about four years at Exeter from new, No. 5571 was transferred to Taunton in 1933 where she remained (apart from a few months at St. Blazey) until well after Nationalisation. (14th May 1936)

At the west end of Taunton station, 'Bulldog' 4—4—0 No. 3443 *Chaffinch* pulls away from the Barnstaple departure bay with the 4.30 p.m. to Barnstaple Junction, which included a through coach from Paddington to Ilfracombe. This engine was transferred from Newton Abbot shed in 1935, remaining at Taunton (and Barnstaple) until her withdrawal in the summer of 1949. The engine at the adjacent platform is 'Castle' 4—6—0 No. 5025 *Chirk Castle*, an Old Oak engine which had just celebrated its second birthday! She had worked in the 1.05 p.m. Swindon train, conveying through coaches from the 10.45 a.m. Paddington service. (14th May 1936)

The 12.30 p.m. Paddington to Weymouth train entering Castle Cary station behind No. 5943 *Elmdon Hall* of Westbury shed. The regular train from Paddington had a dining car section at the head which was detached at Westbury, and on Saturdays conveyed a pair of coaches at the rear to Newbury. On this train, however, there seems to be a diner marshalled in between the regular pair of three-coach 'sets' forming the Weymouth portion. Being a Saturday, perhaps some extra or important custom warranted the extension of its normal journey. (16th May 1936)

'Saint' Class 4—6—0 No. 2971 *Albion* in immaculate condition after an overhaul at Swindon Factory, is seen leaving Platform 2 at Bristol Temple Meads with the empty stock of the 5.00 p.m. Swindon train, bound for Malago Vale carriage sidings. In addition to the four-coach set, she has an extra Third at the rear 'for Evening Trip Passengers'. The 5.00 p.m. was also scheduled to convey a Siphon C from Chippenham (ex Calne) for Crewe and Manchester, which may be seen behind the 'Metro' tank on page 48. *Albion* was allocated to Swindon shed, remaining there until her withdrawal in 1946. In nearby Platform 4, 'Castle' Class No. 5003 *Lulworth Castle*, a Cardiff engine, waits at the head of the 4.30 p.m. Paddington to Weston-Super-Mare Express. (15th May 1936)

'Bulldog' No. 3433 leaving Bristol (Bath Road) shed with a full load of coal in the tender to pick up her next working. She spent most of the 'twenties at Hereford shed, and was allocated to Bath Road in 1931. She was to leave Bristol shortly to spend her last three years' service at Andover Junction and Swindon. The 'Bulldogs' were increasingly being used on goods duties in the late 'thirties, and 3433 may have ended her days on such turns. (15th May 1936)

Another ex-works engine, though far from immaculate, is '47XX' Class 2—8—0 No. 4703 from Laira shed, Plymouth. She is seen here on a running-in turn, the 5.45 p.m. Temple Meads to Swindon (via Badminton). The train consists of a two-coach 'B' set, a load of around 60 tons — less than half the weight of the engine and tender. The fireman would not be unduly taxed on this run! (15th May 1936)

The 'Metro' tanks, 140 of which were built for branch and local duties between 1869 and 1899, were to be found on many parts of the system. Here, one of the 1892 batch, No. 1497, is seen on station pilot duties at Temple Meads on 15th May 1936, one of the forty engines surviving at this time. She was stationed at St. Philip's Marsh from 1936 until her withdrawal in the summer of 1938. The vehicles being conveyed could be the Trowbridge and Manchester parcels van, and the Calne to Crewe Siphon C (Harris's sausage traffic) together with another Siphon C, possibly again from Calne. These were conveyed onwards by the 12.15 p.m. Penzance to Crewe train, due to arrive at Temple Meads some fifteen minutes after this photograph was taken.

A cuckoo in the nest! Southern Railway Class 'U' 2—6—0 No. 1626 (Salisbury) heading the empty stock of the 4.18 p.m. Salisbury (2.05 p.m. ex Portsmouth) to Bristol out of Temple Meads, bound for the carriage sidings at Malago Vale. This was a common sight at Bristol during certain periods, with No. 1626 or her sister engine 1624 working in daily with this train in 1936. The engine would then return to Salisbury with the 8.45 p.m. from Temple Meads, the working being a means of balancing GW engine mileage on the Southern system. The leading van was specified for Post Office mails, and standing at the platform, having been detached from the rear of the train, is the Trowbridge van seen behind the 'Metro' in the photograph above. (15th May 1936)

Standing in Salisbury station, 'Bulldog' 4—4—0 No. 3376 *River Plym* awaiting departure with the 12.42 p.m. to Bristol Temple Meads, on Whit Monday, 17th May 1937. The traditional use of ageing corridor stock on cross-country services may be seen, with 'lavatory stock' (not corridor stock) being specified. The 'non-clerestory' Third was a strengthening vehicle on the set, used daily on the 12.42 p.m. *River Plym* was allocated to Bath Road shed at this time, being moved to Didcot in 1939 to work out the rest of her days. She was withdrawn in September 1948.

One of the numerous and successful 'Dean Goods' Class hurrying down the bank towards Sarnau, a few miles west of Carmarthen on the main line to Fishguard. No. 2404, a resident of Carmarthen shed, was heading an east-bound pick-up freight destined for Carmarthen Junction. Taken into military service as WD 190, she was shipped to France in 1940. There she stayed until 1949, returning to England to be scrapped. (31st May 1937)

'Small Prairie' 2—6—2 Tanks Nos. 4506 and 5539 approaching Saundersfoot station, four miles to the north of Tenby, on a through train from Paddington to Pembroke Dock. The 8.55 a.m. Paddington conveyed through coaches for Swansea, Neyland, and a slip portion for Weston-Super-Mare (slipped at Stoke Gifford) in addition to the three 70ft coaches forming the Pembroke 'train'. The two leading vehicles on the branch train are strengthening from Whitland, followed by the through coaches. In addition, Pembroke Dock received a single through coach on the 11.55 a.m. Paddington train. The three vehicles returned the following morning as the 8.00 a.m. Pembroke Dock to Paddington, whilst the single coach was attached to the 10.50 a.m. departure, being conveyed back to Paddington by the 11.20 a.m. service from Milford Haven. The engines show the difference in tank design between the two series, the earlier 4506 having the flat-topped 1,000-gallon capacity whilst the later engines carried 300 gallons more. No. 4506 was a Whitland engine, alternating between that shed and Pembroke Dock for the rest of her GW career. The '55XX' was from Pembroke Dock shed, moving on to Bristol (Bath Road) in January 1938. (29th May 1937)

'52XX' Class 2–8–0 Tank No. 5226 making good progress on a west-bound 'H' lamp train of laden coal wagons past Bynea, on the Swansea avoiding line via Felin Fran. At this time, 5226 was a Pantyffynon engine, and her load was probably destined for the yards at Llandilo Junction. (31st May 1937).

Former Taff Vale 'O4' Class 0—6—2T No. 278 (ex TVR No. 1) hauling a loaded coal train south-eastwards down the Rhondda Valley. The location is between Porth and Trehafod, and the rake of 'Insoles' wagons in the background are standing on the Eirw branch. No. 278 was allocated to Ferndale, a shed situated on the Porth to Maerdy line, which had a normal complement of around a dozen 0—6—2 Tanks of Taff Vale and Great Western origins. (1st June 1937)

Another ex-Taff Vale 'O4' Class 0–6–2T, this time No. 291 (TVR No. 56) at Tonypandy, west of Porth. The engine retains its original boiler and chimney, but has been fitted with a GW safety valve casing, and modified cab and bunker. Built by Beyer Peacock in 1908, the engine carries a 'C21' target board on its bufferbeam, indicating a Cardiff Cathays mineral turn. The engine came off shed each morning at 9.55, starting work at 10.00 a.m. from Cathays van siding to the Taff Vale section as directed by Control. (1st June 1937)

A heavily 'Swindonised' 'O4' tank No. 299 (ex-TVR No. 98) at Maerdy station with the 12.55 p.m. train to Porth. The 'FA' board indicates a Ferndale shed turn, in this instance a passenger train working. The line was predominantly operated as a branch, with passenger trains running between Maerdy and Porth, connecting at the latter station with the through services running between Cardiff, Pontypridd and Treherbert. In view of the heavy gradients on the branch, up trains to Maerdy were limited to about five coaches for a '56XX', and three or four for the TVR Tanks. (1st June 1937)

Mixed traffic '43XX' 2—6—0 No. 6334 at the head of the 6.20 p.m. Hereford to Pontypool Road stopping train near Tram Inn. The practice of placing the guard's section in the centre of local trains rather than at one end was favoured by many divisions, especially Central Wales. Where only one guard/van section was provided on the train, as in the case above, then it made sense to marshal it centrally, both from an operating and traffic point of view. The engine was from Shrewsbury shed. (2nd June 1937)

'Dean Goods' 0—6—0 No. 2384 approaching Ledbury with the 12.30 p.m. service from Gloucester, consisting of an 1897 low-roof van third (D22), a clerestory corridor composite, and a steel-panelled corridor van third of somewhat later vintage! 2384 was a Gloucester engine, due to spend a short period at Evesham shed before withdrawal in December 1938. (4th June 1937)

Worcester shed's '48XX' 0—4—2 Tank No. 4818 propelling the 3.50 p.m. Malvern Wells to Worcester (Foregate Street) auto-train into Malvern Link station on Friday, 4th June 1937. The unit normally operated ten return trips each day on this service, including one out as far as Ledbury. On Saturdays, a second autocoach was added to the formation.

Bearing the train identification number 523, 'Castle' Class 4—6—0 No. 5027 *Farleigh Castle* passes Pewsey with the 2.20 p.m. (Saturdays only) Minehead to Paddington train. The seven-coach formation specified contained a van third, composite, four thirds and a brake compo, and had worked down that morning to Minehead on the 9.35 a.m. Paddington. The engine, from Old Oak Common, may well have done the same, though it would have been detached at Taunton on the outward journey, and has probably picked up the return train from Norton Fitzwarren. (9th July 1938)

Following the 'Minehead' to Pewsey was the late-running 2.27 p.m. (Saturdays) Bristol to Reading (via Devizes) local passenger. The timetable determined that the local train should precede the express, and be passed by it at Newbury. However, the late running of the local gave it insufficient headway against the express, and it was probably held at Patney & Chirton for the 'Minehead' to take the road. The 2.27 p.m. was running about 20 minutes behind time when photographed, with 'Hall' Class 4—6—0 No. 4914 *Cranmore Hall* (Reading Shed) in charge.

The Saturday 11.10 a.m. Penzance to Paddington Express nears the summit of the climb up from Pewsey Vale at Savernake (Low Level) station behind 'Castle' Class 4–6–0 No. 5055 *Earl of Eldon*. Built in June 1936, 5055 was originally named *Lydford Castle*, until August 1937 when the 'Earl' plates were bestowed upon it. [The *Lydford Castle* nameplates were then transferred onto No. 5079 (1939), being displaced yet again in 1940 by *Lysander*, finally ending up on 7006 (1946).] The engine is seen here working back to its home shed, Old Oak, having worked down to Plymouth the previous evening. The leading coach, a brake composite, was working up from Plymouth, whilst the remaining nine vehicles originated from Penzance. The train in the bay platform is the 5.21 p.m. service to Marlborough with a '4575' tank at the head. (9th July 1938)

Approaching the 'other' Savernake station, High Level (ex-MSWJR), is the 3.05 p.m. Cheltenham to Andover Junction train. 'Bulldog' 4—4—0 No. 3426 of Andover Junction shed hauls the standard three-coach formation allocated to the through services on the line at this time. The brake compo/third/van third combinations ran all of the Cheltenham, Andover Junction and Southampton trains, being strengthened by an extra third when necessary. Would-be MSWJ passengers from Savernake had to read their timetables carefully from the latter 'thirties, as the Low Level station only was tabulated. A letter within the departure time signified that the train left from the High Level station, some 250 yards distant; the through services were utilising both stations! (9th July 1938)

The Wantage Tramway Company's entire locomotive stud stands outside the small engine shed at the Wantage (Mill Street) terminus during the 'thirties. No. 5, a George England & Co. well tank (formerly *Shannon* of the Sandy and Potton Railway) and No. 7, a Manning Wardle design, worked the line until December 1945 when it was closed by order of the Ministry of Transport. No. 5 was preserved by the GWR, and now resides at the Didcot Railway Centre, whilst No. 7 was sold to Messrs. Adams of Newport (Mon). (1st October 1938)

A typical lunch-time scene at Newbury station. Standing at the down platform is the 12.30 p.m. Paddington to Weymouth Express behind 'Star' Class No. 4038 *Queen Berengaria*, from Westbury shed. The Weymouth vehicles are formed at the front of the train, and the Westbury section, including the dining car, at the rear. Departure is imminent, at 1.43 p.m. In the down bay is Old Oak Common 'Hall' No. 5950 *Wardley Hall* with the 12.53 p.m. Reading to Westbury. This train arrived at Newbury at 1.25 p.m., then positioned in the bay to await the departure of the 'Down Weymouth', which it followed at 1.52 p.m. 'Duke' Class 4—4—0 No. 3280 (originally named *Tregenna*) waits on the down through line for her platform to become vacant. She is on the 12.35 p.m. Didcot to Southampton train, which was scheduled to arrive at 1.19 p.m., departing Newbury at 2.00 p.m. The engine worked through from Didcot to Southampton on this service, returning with the 4.55 p.m. Southampton to Didcot. She was withdrawn from service three months after this photograph was taken. Shunting vans in the yard alongside the Lambourn bay (behind the up platform station nameboard) is 'Dean' No. 2535, the Newbury pilot. The Lambourn train itself is waiting at the bay platform for its 2.00 p.m. departure time, behind an unseen ex-MSWJ 2—4—0 No. 1336. The van third is accompanied by a trailer for use at the unstaffed halts. Some ten minutes before the photograph was taken, the 11.22 a.m. Bristol to Paddington (via Devizes) had called at the station up platform, further adding to the activity in what was a very busy hour for the station staff. (24th February 1939)

Yeovil (Pen Mill) station, at lunchtime on Sunday, 21st May 1939, with a 'Castle' Class 4–6–0 No. 5014 *Goodrich Castle*, from Bath Road shed, Bristol, standing at the head of the 10.00 a.m. Temple Meads to Weymouth service. This train normally consisted of just four corridor coaches, one of which in the mid-thirties was an example of the rare buffet van thirds, serving tea, coffee and light refreshments. By 1939, however, that vehicle had gone, leaving the passengers' gastronomic arrangements in their own hands; a normal van third replaced it at the head of the formation. The front of 'Bulldog' No. 3371 can be seen above the tender of the 'Castle'.

'Bulldog' 4–4–0, No. 3371 *Sir Massey Lopes*, shunting milk vehicles at Pen Mill after the departure of the 'Castle'. No. 3371 was a Westbury engine, and had worked the 10.00 a.m. Westbury to Yeovil milk empties, hence the 'C' headlamps. Her next duty was to arrange those empties destined for Thorney, on the branch to Taunton, and depart with them at 1.20 p.m. She returned to Yeovil with the 5.00 p.m. Thorney milk, the vehicles being forwarded on the following 4.30 p.m. Weymouth to Paddington milk train. (Sunday, 21st May 1939)

The 4.07 p.m. Swindon to Laira Junction express freight ('D' Class) passing Keinton Mandeville (about 20 miles east of Taunton) in charge of 'Grange' Class 4–6–0 No. 6814 *Enborne Grange*. Instead of taking the main line route via Bristol, this freight was routed via Chippenham, Trowbridge and Westbury to Taunton. No. 6814 was a truly West Country engine, being allocated to Exeter when new in December 1936 and still shedded there at the time of this photograph. In 1941, she was transferred down to Newton, remaining there until at least the mid-'fifties. (23rd May 1939)

'King' Class 4—6—0 No. 6020 *King Henry IV* about to pass beneath the bridge carrying the Somerset & Dorset Joint line at Cole, Somerset. Like *Enborne Grange*, she was another West Country resident in Great Western days, being a Laira engine from July 1930 until January 1949. She is pictured here at the head of a fitted freight, believed to be the 4.00 p.m. Exeter to Old Oak Common meat. Whilst the 'Kings' were predominantly express passenger engines, they were to be found on 'C' Class parcels or vacuum freights on a regular basis at certain periods, as 'balancing' workings to their primary duties (1st June 1939).

Passing under the Somerset & Dorset bridge at Cole, 'Castle' Class No. 5027 *Farleigh Castle*, from Old Oak shed, heads the 1.30 p.m. (Saturdays only) Paddington to Kingswear Express. Conveying four coaches for Kingswear, and five for Paignton (including a diner), this train acted as a form of relief service to the following 1.40 p.m. Paddington (bound for Penzance). On Mondays to Fridays, the 1.40 p.m. alone ran, conveying vehicles for both Torbay and Penzance. (3rd June 1939)

'Castle' Class 4—6—0 No. 5079 *Lydford Castle*, with the Saturday 3.30 p.m. Paddington train, speeding down the bank from Brewham Summit towards Bruton on 3rd June 1939. This engine, barely a month old when this photograph was taken, was allocated to Old Oak Common shed. She carries the 'mobile' nameplates, *Lydford Castle*, originally fitted to 'Castle' 5055. In January 1941, No. 5079 was re-named *Lysander*, the Lydford plates moving on yet again to eventually find a permanent home on the 1946 'Castle', No. 7006. The 3.30 p.m. Paddington was the last of the daily Down West Country expresses to use the Berks and Hants route, the later services all being routed via Bristol. The first four coaches (van third, third, first, van third) form the regular Penzance portion, and are followed by a strengthening coach (a 'Dreadnought' third). Then follow the two regular (roof boarded) Plymouth North Road vehicles, a dining car and brake compo. The last five vehicles are all destined for Kingswear; two thirds for strengthening, then the regular coaches (third, first, and van third). On Mondays to Fridays, the 3.30 p.m. terminated at Truro.

A Westbury 'Hall', No. 5968 *Cory Hall* passing under the Somerset & Dorset line bridge at Cole on her way down the bank to Castle Cary, some two miles distant. She is hauling the 12.30 p.m. Paddington to Weymouth Express, normally consisting of six coaches by this stage of the journey, but perhaps with one or two additional thirds at the rear to accommodate extra Saturday travellers. (3rd June 1939)

The unmistakeable 'KGV', No. 6000 *King George V* of Old Oak shed, pictured near Cole with the train perhaps most associated with her, the 'Cornish Riviera Express'. This is the Up service, the 10.00 a.m. from Penzance, running non-stop from Exeter to Paddington. During the winter schedule (current at the time of the photograph), the destination boards of the Down 'Riviera' read like a Who`s Who of West Country resorts, but the Up train was slightly more conservative. Behind the engine is a brake compo (plus two strengthening vehicles) that had been attached to the train with the loco at Plymouth North Road. Further brake composites from St. Ives, Newquay, Falmouth, and Exeter were also conveyed, with the main six-coach Penzance portion of 'Centenary' stock (including the twin dining unit) being marshalled towards the rear of the train.

Three miles to the south of Yeovil, on the line to Weymouth, was Thornford Bridge Halt. Churchward '43XX' Mogul No. 6358, from Weymouth shed, is seen here passing the staggered platforms with an empty stock working on Sunday, 4th June 1939. If such a train was capable of maintaining express passenger timings, it was given Class 'A' status, as may be seen by the headlamps on this one. No. 6358 spent about three years at Weymouth, being transferred to Swindon shed shortly after the photograph was taken. The unprotected Tilley lamp on the station nameboard would not last long in these vandalistic days!

'Hall' Class 4–6–0 No. 5949 *Trematon Hall* pauses at Yeovil (Pen Mill) station with the 5.03 p.m. Bristol to Weymouth stopping passenger train. The engine is working home to Weymouth with a four-coach corridor set forming her train. This service called at all nine stations to Dorchester (GW), then Upwey Junction and Weymouth, taking a little over an hour to cover the remaining 27 miles. (26th July 1939)

The 5.55 p.m. Taunton to Yeovil train arriving at Pen Mill's Up Platform behind a Taunton 'Dean Goods' No. 2527. This engine would shortly be taken into military service as WD No. 150, and sent to France. The train consists of the inevitable 'B' set, which had run through from Minehead (departing 4.25 p.m.) with a thirty-minute wait at Taunton en route. (26th July 1939)

The 'Dean' repositioned her stock in the Down Platform after the departure of the 'Hall', and visited the shed to turn. Here she is awaiting departure time, scheduled at 7.33 p.m., for the return journey to Taunton. Standing in the Up Platform can be seen the 6.20 p.m. Weymouth to Bristol service, which was due to depart a couple of minutes after the 'Dean' and her train. The auto-coach on the right was used on the Pen Mill to Yeovil Town service, which was shared with the Southern Railway. The Southern carried out two return journeys with their push-pull set (No. 659), whilst GW autos carried out four. (26th July 1939)

Hendford Halt was situated on the western outskirts of Yeovil, about 1½ miles from Pen Mill station on the line to Taunton. The halt was opened in the early 'thirties, but a goods yard had existed there from the opening of the line, in 1853. The junction for the siding into the Westland works can be seen in the distance. Here '45XX' Prairie No. 5521 is entering the halt with the 2.15 p.m. from Taunton. Like several other trains on this branch, the stock had worked through from Minehead, and in this instance, the 'B' set would return to Taunton with the engine as the 3.55 p.m. from Pen Mill. No. 5521 herself had a long association with Taunton shed, arriving there from Newton Abbot in 1930 for a stay of over twenty years. (11th August 1939)

The 1.30 p.m. Penzance to Paddington Express waiting at Taunton behind 'King' Class 4—6—0 No. 6019 *King Henry V*. Originally a Wolverhampton (Stafford Road) engine, 6019 was transferred to Laira in June 1935 and remained there until after nationalisation. She has just been re-coupled to her train, having taken off a brake van destined for Birmingham. The leading vehicles form part of the five-coach portion from Penzance, with a dining car marshalled second in the formation. Further back was a three-coach set from Paignton, and attached to the rear at this stop was a through coach from Ilfracombe. The train will run non-stop to Paddington. (15th August 1939)

'Bulldog' 4—4—0 No. 3443 *Chaffinch* at work as station pilot at Taunton on Tuesday, 15th August 1939. Much of her work was done on the Barnstaple branch from the mid-'thirties, and she spent short periods at Barnstaple shed itself. The token exchange mounting on the front edge of the tender was for use on the Minehead and Barnstaple branches. With the introduction of automatic token exchanging apparatus on those branches, some thirty-five of Taunton's engines were fitted with the mechanism, involving members of the '2251', 'Dean Goods', '43XX', '45XX' and '51XX' Classes, in addition to the 'Bulldogs'. The speed of trains was not to exceed 40 mph when exchanging tokens by the automatic apparatus.

Propelling wagons outside Taunton Goods is '2021' Class 0—6—0PT No. 2050, one of four engines normally employed each day on yard duties. The engine seems to have spent virtually all of its fifty-three years life in the West Country, being at St. Blazey in 1902, Bodmin in 1914, drifting gradually eastwards as far as Taunton (from where it was frequently outstationed at Bridgwater) by the late 'thirties, before returning to Cornwall in 1941. She ended her career at St. Blazey in 1951. (15th August 1939)

Auto train services around Taunton were operated by three units: one from Taunton, running in a two-day cycle with a Frome auto, plus a second Frome unit making visits to Taunton during the day. The services encompassed visits to Bridgwater, Wellington, and Wiveliscombe (on the Barnstaple line), but the bulk of them ran between Taunton and Castle Cary. Taunton 'Metro' tank No. 3582 with an empty autocoach is running wrong line towards the station, to form the 6.55 p.m. departure for Castle Cary and Frome. The 'King' from the 1.30 p.m. Penzance, with a van it has removed from that train (see page 76) can be seen to the rear of the autocoach. (15th August 1939)

'Star' Class 4–6–0 No. 4015 *Knight of St. John* entering Taunton station with the 5.50 p.m. Bristol Temple Meads to Taunton stopping train (despite the 'A' headlamps!). The four corridor coaches form an 'M' set (van third, 'lavatory compo', third, and van third), and will continue on from Taunton as the 8.20 p.m. to Newton Abbot, normally behind an Exeter '55XX' tank. No. 4015 was an Old Oak engine for many years, taking the principal West Country and Birmingham line services out of Paddington. When 'Castles' began to appear in numbers, she moved initially to South Wales, for the London trains, then eventually to Bath Road for services in the London, Shrewsbury and Plymouth directions. Her final move was in 1940, when she was transferred to Swindon shed for the last eleven years of her working life. (15th August 1939)

Moreton Cutting yard, Didcot, with one of the later '38XX' Class 2—8—0s, No. 3859 (built in October 1942), easing out of the sidings and onto the Up relief line with an 'H' Class freight on Sunday, 15th September 1946. No. 3859 spent her Great Western days at Southall shed, working such trains as the 2.05 a.m. to Cardiff, the 5.50 a.m. to Severn Tunnel Junction, and the 4.00 a.m. (Sundays) Severn Tunnel Junction to West Drayton (or Hanwell Bridge, Acton, or Old Oak, depending upon the load!), which is most probably the train pictured.

Clad in typical Austerity grime, 'Hall' Class 4–6–0 No. 5958 *Knolton Hall* passes a PW gang at Steventon with the late-running 8.50 a.m. (Sundays) Old Oak Common to Carmarthen Junction fitted freight. The 'Hall', which appears to have had its buffer beam number crudely chalked in, was a Cardiff engine, and would call at Swindon (to change engine crews), Stoke Gifford and Severn Tunnel Junction on its way west. The train was carefully marshalled, with vacuum vehicles in the leading part bound for Carmarthen, Llanelly, Swansea, Neath, Port Talbot, Bridgend, Cardiff and Severn Tunnel Junction, followed by non-vacuum wagons in the reverse order. The load was scheduled to 'equal 65 ten-ton wagons in length as far as Severn Tunnel Junction', which would seem to be the case in this instance. (3rd November 1946)

'Dean Goods' 0–6–0 No. 2573 (RDG) leaving Newbury with the 2.00 p.m. service to Lambourn, consisting of the traditional autocoach and van third combination. The branch at this time was worked mostly by a Reading diesel railcar, though the steam unit was used to cover unavailability (etc), with Reading shed supplying the engine. The freight on the adjacent Up Main is probably the 1.45 a.m. Tavistock Junction to Banbury (if running to time!), which took the DN & S route via Compton to Didcot. (23rd March 1948)

Departing from Newbury on Friday, 12th March 1948 is 'Hall' Class 4—6—0 No. 5925 *Eastcote Hall* on the 12.43 p.m. Reading to Westbury train. Like its pre-war counterpart, this train had a lengthy wait at Newbury to allow the 12.30 p.m. Paddington to Weymouth Express to overtake it (see pages 62/3). No. 5925 is a Westbury engine on a return working, having brought the 6.48 a.m. from Westbury to Reading that morning. The first three coaches (a pair of thirds and a brake compo, corridor stock) were also part of that train, which included empty stock, too. At the rear, a 'B' set allocated to Frome is also working home, having formed the 9.03 a.m. Frome to Reading earlier that day.

Bearing the train identification number 165, the 10.40 a.m. (Saturdays only) Paddington to Kingswear Express passes through Newbury station behind 'Star' Class 4—6—0 No. 4028 (formerly *King John*, name removed in 1927, and *Roumanian Monarch*, name removed 1940). She is a Westbury engine, obviously 'roped in' to help with the summer Saturday rush, and survived in traffic until late 1951. The train normally consisted of ten coaches for Kingswear, and three more at the rear for Paignton. (30th July 1949)

Allocated to Banbury shed in July 1947, ex-WD Austerity 2—8—0 No. 77297 is passing Enborne Junction, Newbury, with the 1.45 a.m. Tavistock Junction to Banbury Class 'J' freight. Running via the Newbury and Didcot line, this freight arrived at Banbury around 6.30 p.m. that evening, having been on the road for nearly seventeen hours. In addition to calling at Newton Abbot, Exeter, Taunton and Westbury en route, she was scheduled to stop a further seventeen times for bank engines, crew changes, examination and traffic purposes. (13th May 1948)

Running eight minutes ahead of train No. 165 (on the opposite page) through Newbury was the 10.35 a.m. (Saturdays only) Paddington to Penzance, the second part of the 10.30 a.m. Paddington ('Cornish Riviera'). This service conveyed coaches for Penzance and Falmouth, the normal load being thirteen. 'Castle' Class 4—6—0 No. 5040 Stokesay Castle of Old Oak shed will be in charge of the train as far as Plymouth (North Road). (30th July 1949)

In the early stages of the war, the London Division of the GWR 'rationalised' its coach formations for suburban services with the introduction of the 'Q' set. These were either five-coach non-corridor sets (a standard four-coach set plus an extra third) or six-coach ex 'Local C' sets, all of which were third class only. Any first class compartments were paper-labelled 'Third class'. Corridor vehicles found their way into the formations, too, as can be seen in this photograph of the 9.45 a.m. Reading (10.40 a.m. Didcot) to Oxford train, leaving Radley station on the last leg of its journey. The 'Q' set has an extra vehicle added at the rear, and is being hauled by 'Saint' Class 4–6–0 No. 2933 *Bibury Court* of Leamington shed. The 'Saint' had left Leamington with the 6.45 a.m. to Oxford, continued to Didcot with the 8.52 a.m., then started her return journey with the 10.40 a.m. from Didcot. (15th May 1948)

The Saturday 10.40 a.m. Oxford to Didcot stopping train approaching Radley station on 15th May 1948. The formation includes three extra vehicles positioned at the head, with the four-coach set and the three trailing coaches forming the regular Saturday train. No. 6312, on arrival at Didcot, will take up passenger shunting duties as the west end pilot until 6.30 p.m., after which it will work to its home shed, Reading, with the 6.55 p.m. passenger train.

One of Oxford's three '61XX' tanks, No. 6103, arriving at Radley station with the 6.20 p.m. Oxford to Reading local train. The five-coach 'Q' set has an extra vehicle at the rear, and is making its way back to Paddington. At Didcot, the '61XX' would hand over the train to the '43XX' 2–6–0, No. 6312 (seen in the previous photograph) for the continuation to Reading, whilst she would return to Oxford with the 8.05 p.m. local passenger. (15th May 1948)

86

Activity at Oxford North with the 10.15 a.m. Oxford (Rewley Road) to Bletchley passing the junction connecting the ex-LMS line with the ex-GW, worked by a pair of 4F 2—6—0s, recently built at Horwich and now stationed at Bletchley. The engines are Nos. 3005 and 3003, each carrying the short-lived 'M' prefix to its number. A grimy 'Hall' stands on the adjacent Western Region Down Main, possibly having worked the 9.48 a.m. Didcot to Oxford Fast, now marshalling the empty stock. (19th May 1948)

'Castle' Class 4—6—0 No. 5017 *St. Donats Castle* emerging from Sonning Cutting with the 1.45 p.m. Paddington to Stourbridge Junction train. No. 5017, allocated to Worcester in 1939, was one of the six 'Castles' at that shed at the time of nationalisation. She had worked up during the morning from Worcester with the 6.50 a.m. Wolverhampton train, and is returning with the 1.45 p.m. The train comprised sections for Wolverhampton (though advertised to Stourbridge Junction only), Hereford, and Birmingham (via Banbury, detached at Oxford). (19th August 1948)

Approaching the opposite end of Sonning Cutting, No. 7016 *Chester Castle* brings the 8.15 a.m. Neyland to Paddington train past Woodley Bridge signal box on the Up Main. She was barely a month old at the time of this photograph, and was allocated to Cardiff (Canton) shed. Her train conveys coaches from Swansea (five, including a dining car), Neyland (five) and Pembroke Dock (three), due into Paddington at 3.40 p.m. (25th August 1948)

Ex-LMS Class G2a (7F) 0—8—0 No. 8952 approaches Oxford station with a transfer freight from Oxford South yard, comprising empty coal wagons. The engine is allocated to Bletchley, and will probably be working back there via Yarnton with one of the goods or 'empties' trains. Departing from the Up Platform is an unidentified 'Hall' (probably from Oxford shed) with the 2.40 p.m. service to Paddington via Thame, Princes Risborough and the GW/GC line, direct to Paddington. Some of these services used the Greenford & Ealing loop, others taking an even more leisurely route via High Wycombe and Maidenhead! (18th September 1948)

One of Old Oak Common's numerous stud of 0—6—0 pannier tanks, No. 8767, taking a lengthy 'H' Class up freight past Oxford Station North Signal Box. The train may be a transfer trip between Yarnton or Oxford North and Hinksey, although the 'H' lamps indicate something of more importance. The only scheduled freight of that class through Oxford at that time of day was the 10.25 a.m. Bordesley to Moreton Cutting. Has the pannier picked up that train for the last part of its journey? (18th September 1948)

'Hall' Class 4—6—0 No. 6912 *Helmster Hall*, about to depart from the Up Platform at Oxford station with the 2.56 p.m. train to Southampton (via the DN & S line) which it will work as far as Didcot. A Bristol (St. Philip's Marsh) engine from new (in March 1941), 6912 had been transferred to Weymouth shed in May 1948. She still carries the train identification number of her previous working, 310, the 10.25 a.m. Weymouth to Wolverhampton train which she brought as far as Oxford. From Didcot, she will work an evening passenger service to Swindon. (18th September 1948)

Easing off the Worcester line and onto the Up Relief at Wolvercote Junction is 'Grange' Class 4—6—0 No. 6802 *Bampton Grange*, at the head of the 10.25 a.m. Bordesley Junction to Moreton Cutting or Reading freight. Rather than use the direct route via Banbury, this train has run via Henley-in-Arden, Stratford-on-Avon, Honeybourne south loop and Moreton-in-Marsh. This seemingly roundabout route was in fact only seven miles longer than via Banbury, and was frequently used by slower traffic in order to keep the main line clear. No. 6802, from Reading shed, is returning home on the balancing duty to the 10.10 a.m. Reading West to Bordesley empties, which she worked the previous day. She spent the night at Tyseley shed. (25th September 1948)

'54XX' Class autotank No. 5413 pauses with the 2.30 p.m. Oxford to Blenheim & Woodstock auto at Wolvercote Junction, to deliver supplies to the signalman on duty. The branch had been worked primarily by '517' Class tanks (including *Fair Rosamund*) until 1947, when 5413 arrived from Southall to take up duties. The '54XXs', from their introduction, were mainly Southall engines, about half the class being shedded there. Both Banbury and the Westbury area also had allocations. Apart from the odd engines stationed in the Swansea and Plymouth Districts, and latterly Oxford, too, those allocations remained much the same in GW days. (25th September 1948)

Eynsham station, on the Fairford branch, Saturday, 25th September 1948, with 2–4–0 'Metro' tank No. 3562 pausing with the 3.35 p.m. Oxford to Carterton service, a 5-coach 'Q' set forming the train. For this set, the Carterton run was a means of 'filling in' between its 12.10 p.m. Paddington to Oxford and 6.40 p.m. Oxford to Paddington duties. The engine would complete two return journeys between Fairford and Oxford, plus the Carterton turn from and to Oxford, in the course of its day's work. No. 3562 came late to Oxford, in February 1948, to work its last twelve months on the Fairford trains, alongside another survivor, No. 3588. 'Metro' tanks had been associated with the Fairford line for many years, No. 1499 working the branch as early as 1901. There were three of the class there by 1914, and six were in use on the line by the time of grouping, that number remaining more or less static until the mid-'forties when scrapping rapidly reduced the survivors. No. 3588 was withdrawn in December 1949, the last of the class, thus severing a long and successful association with the Fairford branch. The concrete platform (erected during World War II) has been preserved, and currently serves at the Great Western Society's Railway Centre at Didcot.

ACKNOWLEDGEMENTS

Firstly I must express my indebtedness to John Copsey for his valuable help in researching the captions, also to Paul Karau for his sound advice on the selection of pictures and their layout. Much of the information on locomotives is drawn from the definitive RCTS publication *Locomotives of the Great Western Railway* and is gratefully acknowledged.

It is largely due to the encouragement of the Great Western Society that this book has seen the light of day and it is therefore proposed to donate a proportion of the proceeds from the sale of the book to the Didcot Railway Centre Museum Library Building Fund.